HOW YOU ARE ASSESSED AT GCSE

Assessment objectives

A01	Demonstrate knowledge and understanding of socio[...] evidence and methods.
A02	Apply knowledge and understanding of sociological theories, concepts, evidence and methods.
A03	Analyse and evaluate sociological theories, concepts, evidence and methods in order to construct arguments, make judgements and draw conclusions.

Paper 1: 1hr 45 mins. Worth 50% of GCSE grade

- The sociology of families
- The sociology of education
- Relevant areas of social theory and methodology

Paper 2: 1 hr 45 mins. Worth 50% of GCSE

- The sociology of crime and deviance
- The sociology of social stratification
- Relevant areas of social theory and methodology

1 RESEARCH DESIGN

What is research?

In the box below, define what is meant by research:

Why might sociologists choose to conduct research?

What might sociologists choose to research?

Why do sociologists conduct research?

Sociologists conduct research for several reasons. Firstly, they conduct research in order to understand the social world by investigating concepts, ideas and behaviours. Their research usually looks to further our understanding of society and the individuals within it. However, a second function of research is to provide empirical evidence to back up their ideas and enable other sociologists to check their work and improve its credibility. This means that sociological research can go on to inform social policies set out by governments.

There is a series of questions a sociologist needs to consider before conducting research.

What area of society do they want to investigate?

What are the aims of the research?

Do they want the research to be scientific?

Do they want to investigate large sections of society or small groups and individuals?

Do they want to be able to apply their findings to the wider population?

What type of data are they looking to collect?

What research method do they want to use?

How might they present their findings to other sociologists?

These questions are answered during the design phase of research. This is where researchers will pick a topic area to investigate, decide on the aims and/or hypothesis of their research, operationalise concepts, decide on their methodological preference and what data they wish to collect. It is also the phase of research where the researcher selects a method to collect the data and run a pilot study to ensure that the method they have chosen is going to collect the data they require. They must also consider the practical, ethical and theoretical issues they might encounter when using their chosen method to investigate their chosen topic area.

Following the design phase, sociologists conduct the research, collecting and interpreting the data. This may be followed by further research before finally being presented to another sociologist for them to conduct a peer review. This is where other sociologists would check over the research for errors or bias. Their research may then be published in academic journals or books and their research could be replicated by others in the future to test the findings of the research.

IDENTIFYING A PROBLEM

Social issues

One of the first concerns of a sociologist when conducting research is selecting the topic that they wish to investigate. As one of the main aims of sociological research is to advance our understanding of contemporary society, many sociologists choose to focus on social issues that are of relevance to wider society. These social issues may be long-standing, such as levels of crime, poverty or inequality between groups. They may also be emerging social issues that need greater understanding, such as the re-emergence of hate crimes, cyber-bulling or environmental damage.

Using your knowledge of contemporary society, identify two issues that you would choose to investigate and explain why you believe these issues to be important.

Social Issue:

Why is it important to understand this issue?

Continues on next page

Social Issue:

Why is it important to understand this issue?

Part of this process may also involve looking at other research that has been conducted in this field of study. This is known as a literature review and helps sociologists to understand some of the explanations for the social issues, as well as highlighting some of the methods that have been used to investigate these issues by other researchers.

Research aims

Once a researcher has chosen the social issue that they wish to study, they must identify suitable aims for their research.

> **Aims:** The aims of sociological research are the purposes that a sociologist has for conducting the research in the first place. In stating the aims of the research, the sociologist is explaining what they want to achieve and how they will achieve it. It allows those that read the research to judge how effective the researcher was in achieving their goal.

Aims of the research should be clear and appropriate for the topic that a sociologist is researching. The aims of the research should also enhance our knowledge of the social world and provide explanations for why things happen. For example, a sociologist looking to research the impact of poverty on the life chances of people in the UK should explain that they are looking for reasons why a lack of resources impacts on a person's education, health, career prospects, and relationships with others.

How research is funded

Sociologists require funding in order to complete their research. Some methods can be quite expensive or take a long time to complete. Other methods may require specialist training and equipment and so sociologists must look to secure funding from one of a range of sources.

Government funding: Governments have a responsibility to research any new social policies they are looking to introduce so that they are aware of the impact that the proposed changes have on their citizens. Governments also conduct research to inform their future planning. For example, an increase in the birth rate may mean that the government would have to allocate more funding for schools. Furthermore, if more students are being identified with specific learning needs, they may have to cut money from other budgets to supply this. They will employ researchers to investigate the reasons for these changes. As governments often require the public's consent, they look for research that will provide them with policies that are popular with the electorate.

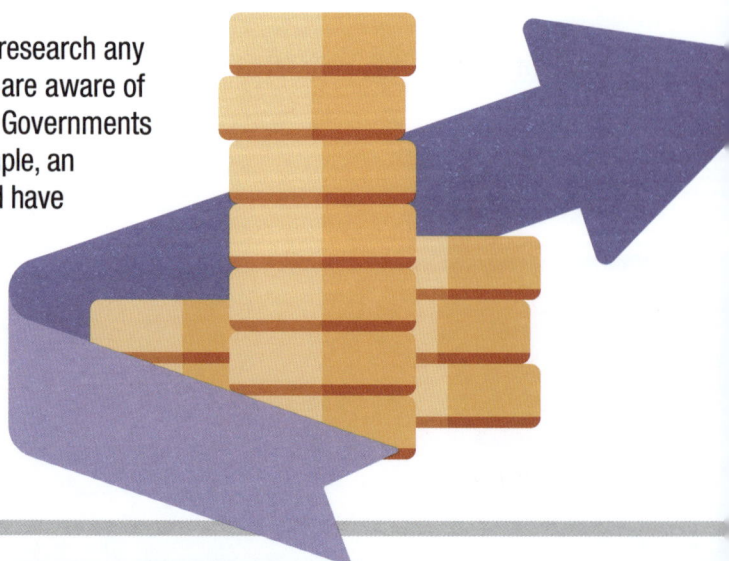

Universities: Universities are one of the biggest sources of research funding in the UK as it is the role of universities to expand the existing knowledge we have. Universities also look to fund research that is ground-breaking and innovative, as this will enhance their reputation and attract more students. Universities will often have specific areas that they wish to focus on and will fund research that improves their knowledge in that area. For example, a university that specialises in gender studies or research into education, may fund research into the reasons for differences in male and female achievement in education.

Businesses: Businesses may fund some forms of sociological research, particularly into the buying and consumption habits of people, or into the relationships between people in the workplace. A famous example of research conducted in a workplace was Elton Mayo's research into the Hawthorne Electricity Company, which found that when workers were observed, their behaviour changed, and they became more productive. This gives us the term **'The Hawthorne Effect'** in sociological research.

Charities: Charities will fund research into areas of interest to that specific charity. For example, the Rowntree Foundation investigates the impacts of poverty in the UK. Charities will conduct this research for several reasons. Firstly, to raise awareness of issues and attract contributions from those that wish to help. Secondly, to understand where their help is needed most, which allows them to allocate resources effectively.

Each of these has its own areas of interest and will fund projects that benefit the institution and those that use it. Therefore, the topic chosen for research may influence who the researcher can obtain funding from. In the table below, **suggest** one type of funding source for the research and **explain** why a sociologist might choose that source.

Aim of research	Funding body	Explanation
To look at the impact of government cuts to public services on people who receive disability benefits		
To research the social media usage of teenagers		
To examine the impact of changes in the role of women on the aspirations of girls in education		
To examine reasons for increases in childhood obesity in the UK		

SELECT A RESEARCH METHOD

Once sociologists have decided on a topic, created their aims and sought approval for their research they must select a method for obtaining data or information that will allow them to make judgements on the aims of their research. There are two considerations sociologists face when selecting a method to conduct their research.

1 Primary sources or secondary sources?

Sociologists have a choice of using either primary or secondary sources in their research. Primary sources are a form of data that is collected by the researcher or members of their team. Examples of primary source are questionnaires, interviews and observations. Secondary sources refers to data that already exists and has usually been compiled by another researcher. Examples of secondary source are official and unofficial statistics, personal documents, historical documents, journals, articles and other media sources. These may or may not have been produced for the purposes of sociological research.

Both sources have their advantages and disadvantages. Further discussion of primary and secondary sources is in **section 4** of this booklet.

2 Quantitative or qualitative data?

A second choice that sociologists face when deciding on a research method is what type of data do they want to collect? Different research methods will produce different types of data, and their choice is often determined by their theoretical preference.

Sociologists who prefer a **positivist** methodology, one which looks to study society in a scientific way, are more likely to choose methods that produce **quantitative data**.

> **Quantitative data** is data that is represented in the form of numerical data. Quantitative data can be drawn from responses to closed questions, could be collected through opinion polls measuring intentions, or through statistics such as census data.

As it is numerical, quantitative data can easily be analysed and trends and patterns established. It is seen as being objective, as sociologists do not apply their own understanding to the data and merely draw conclusions from the numbers they are presented with. It is seen as being more objective (without bias). Methods that collect quantitative data are more structured in their design and can be repeated easily with other participants. For example, closed questionnaires can be distributed to large numbers of people at the same time through the post or email, and the same questionnaire can be repeated with another sample later.

Other sociologists who prefer an **interpretivist** methodology, one that looks to understand the meanings and motivations of individuals, are more likely to choose **qualitative data**.

> **Qualitative data** is data tends to be in the form of text, describing opinions, views, motivations or meanings of the people that are researched. Qualitative data is not numerical and can be difficult to use to make generalisations about society, but offers researchers more insight into the lives of those they study.

Qualitative data is more likely to reflect opinions rather than facts and is criticised by some, as sociologists often draw their own conclusions on what respondents mean in unstructured interviews or when they are being observed. It is not as easily generalised to the population as quantitative data, but sociologists who prefer an interpretivist methodology suggest that researchers need to understand the meanings and motivations behind people's behaviour. They argue that people are different and will have a differing worldview and the role of a sociological researcher is to understand why they hold those views, rather than simply to document them. Qualitative data has high validity but is not easily replicated. For example, two people may have very differing experiences of their education, which means conclusions drawn by a sociologist investigating the first person may not be applicable to the second person. This makes qualitative data less scientific.

The choice of data required by a researcher will influence the methods they choose. Below is a summary of the methods sociologists use and the types of data they produce. These methods will be examined in further detail in section 2 of this workbook.

Quantitative Data	Qualitative Data
Attitude surveys, such as opinion polls	Written questionnaires with open-ended questions
Questionnaires with closed questions, such as mailed or postal questionnaires	Unstructured interviews
Structured interviews	Semi-structured interviews
Structured non-participant observations	Participant and non-participant observations that are unstructured
Laboratory (lab) or controlled experiments	Personal documents
Field experiments	Historical documents
Natural experiments	Journal articles or previous research
Official and non-official statistics	Media sources, such as documentaries, newspapers, magazines, TV shows

It must be noted that some methods can be altered to produce different forms of data. For example, field experiments usually would produce quantitative data, but can also be adapted to produce qualitative data. Furthermore, some sociologists look to adopt a **mixed methods approach** to get a better all-round understanding of a social issue. This involves combining two or more methods to increase the reliability and validity of their research.

Using the definitions above, identify whether the following sources of data are quantitative or qualitative.

Data source	Type of Data
Diary entries of a politician, commenting on changes in attitudes in society	
School league tables	
Trends in birth rate over the past 50 years	
Transcripts of interviews with women about their experiences of raising children	
Rates of re-offending for criminals released from prison	
Photographs from fashion magazines demonstrating different ways women are objectified in the media	
Opinion polls on who people will vote for in next general election	

Forming Hypotheses

Hypothesis: A hypothesis is an informed prediction by the researcher of what their research will prove. The research will look to test the hypothesis proposed by the researcher.

Once a researcher has selected their method, they need to formulate a hypothesis, or an informed prediction, that they will test by conducting their research. The ability to prove or disprove a hypothesis is one of the features of the scientific method. However, abstract concepts such as education, family, crime, beliefs and media are difficult to measure. These concepts need to be **operationalised** so that sociologists can measure the impact of one **variable** on another.

> **Variables:** A variable is any factor that can be controlled, changed, or measured in an experiment. The two types of variables that sociologists are concerned with when doing research are the **independent variable** and the **dependent variable.** The independent variable is the one condition that you change in an experiment. The dependent variable is the variable that you measure or observe. The dependent variable gets its name because it is the factor that is dependent on the state of the independent variable.

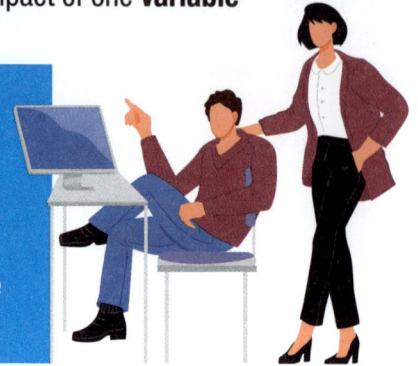

Operationalising Variables

In order to be able to change or measure the variables, they need to be operationalised. This means to define it so that it can be measured and/or expressed quantitatively or qualitatively.

How would you define the concepts below so that they could be measured?

Concept	How would you measure this?
Level of education	
Health	
Religious beliefs	
Media usage	
Criminal activity	
Wealth	
Standard of living	
Representations of women in media	

Conducting a pilot study

> **Pilot Studies:** When conducting research, it is important to make sure that the method a researcher is using is appropriate to use to collect the data required. Researchers, therefore, often trial their research using small-scale pilot studies, which are a 'rehearsal' of the final piece of research. By using these pilot studies, any errors can be corrected before data collection begins.

Before a sociologist conducts their research, they will conduct a pilot study to test out their hypothesis, ensure that the method they are using is appropriate for collecting the type of data they require and make sure that they identify any issues that they may not have considered when designing their research. Conducting a pilot study on a small scale allows sociologists to correct any errors before they begin their research. If, for example, a sociologist sent out 10,000 questionnaires and found that one of the questions was too difficult for people to understand or caused distress amongst participants, this would be a waste of time and resources. Therefore, conducting a small-scale study beforehand helps the researcher to identify any practical or ethical issues and correct them, improving the validity and reliability of their research.

On the following page is an example of a questionnaire that has multiple errors in it. Read through the questionnaire and correct these errors.

HEALTH AND LIFESTYLE QUESTIONNAIRE

The purpose of this questionnaire is to investigate lifestyle choices and how they impact on people's health and well-being. Please answer as honestly as you can. All your information will be kept in accordance with GDPR guidelines.

1 What is your age?

A 13- 18 ☐
B 18-25 ☐
C 25-45 ☐
D 45-65 ☐
E Over 65 ☐

2 What is your BMI?

☐ (box)

3 Which of the following would you classify yourself as?

A Seriously obese ☐
B Obese ☐
C Overweight ☐
D Average ☐
E Below average ☐

4 Do you smoke?

A Yes ☐
B No ☐

5 When do you smoke?

A In the morning ☐
B After meals ☐
C In the evening ☐
D When drinking ☐
E Before bed ☐

6 How much do you smoke?

A A little ☐
B About average ☐
C A lot ☐
D Occasionally ☐

7 Do you think that smoking is bad for your health? If so, why?

☐ (box)

8 How many calories do you consume daily?

A 0-1000 ☐
B 1000-2000 ☐
C 1500-2500 ☐
D 2000-3000 ☐
E Over 3000 ☐

9 How often do you eat 'fast food'?

A Daily ☐
B Twice a week ☐
C Three times a week ☐
D Less than once a week ☐
E Never ☐

10 How tired do you feel?

A Very ☐
B A little ☐
C Not very tired ☐
D Feel awake ☐

11 Do you think that people who eat fast food and smoke should pay for their healthcare?

☐ (box)

Questions continue on next page

12	How often do you drink alcohol?	
	A	Daily	☐
	B	2-3 times a week	☐
	C	Almost every day	☐
	D	Once a week	☐

13 Does alcohol impact on your mental health?

14	Have you in the past had any thoughts of self-harm?	
	A	Regularly	☐
	B	Once or twice	☐
	C	Never	☐

Thank you for taking part in this questionnaire.

Finding a Sample

When conducting research, sociologists must select a **target population** that they wish to study. Often this population is too large to study at one time. For example, if a sociologist wanted to research the educational background of students studying GCSE Sociology, they would have to research over 16,000 students. This is not practical due to the costs and time it would take, so instead they choose a sample of the target population to study.

A sample is a smaller section of the population that is selected for research purposes as trying to collect data from the entire target population would be unmanageable. The target population is organised into a sampling frame – or list of potential participants – and the researcher will select the sample using one of several sampling methods. These methods can be representative of the population or unrepresentative.

Representative Sampling Methods

A representative sample is a sample that includes a wide range of characteristics that are seen in the general population. Representative samples are more likely to be able to draw conclusions from and generalise to the wider population. Representative methods are more likely to be used in large-scale research. Examples include: **random sampling**, **stratified sampling**.

Unrepresentative Sampling Methods

When a sample that takes part in a study is not representative of the target population, and therefore anything learned from them, cannot be used to generalise to others outside of the study. For example, only women used in a study. Unrepresentative sampling is often used for hard to reach groups or when the sociologist is focusing on the experience of a specific group in society. Examples include: **snowball sampling**, **opportunity sampling**.

Target Population (all students studying GCSE Sociology)

Sampling Frame (students at one school studying GCSE Sociology)

Sample (a selection of students taken from sampling frame)

The table below contains brief summaries of each of the different sampling methods.

Sample type	Description
Cluster sample	Sampling method wherein the members of the population are selected at random, from naturally occurring groups called 'clusters'. For example, if in the target population students from year 9, 10 and 11 were present, the researcher would organise these into 3 clusters and select participants from each of the 3 groups.
Opportunity sample	An opportunity sample is obtained by asking members of the population of interest if they would take part in your research. An example of this would be to ask students studying GCSE Sociology if they wanted to take part.
Quota sample	The researcher looks to include a certain number of people from a range of categories.
Random sample	Every person on the sampling frame has an equal chance of being selected for the research. This is seen as representative as names are either simply drawn from a hat or allocated by a random number generator.
Snowball sample	The researcher approaches one person who meets the criteria for their research and is introduced to others who have a similar experience by the research participant. These additional participants then introduce the researcher to further participants. The effect is like a snowball rolling down a hill, gathering more and more information as the researcher is introduced to more potential participants.
Systematic sample	Involves choosing every nth name from a list to create an unbiased sample to take part in research. An example of this would be taking the name of every third student on a register to take part in the research.

One way that students can remember the differences between sampling methods is by drawing a visual representation of that sample. **In the spaces below, illustrate each of the sampling methods without using words.**

Cluster sample	Opportunity sample

Random sample	Snowball sample

Continues on next page

Systematic sample	Quota sample

CONDUCTING RESEARCH

Practical considerations

Practical considerations relate to time, money and logistics. Sometimes the best method for researching a particular topic, theoretically, has to be rejected because it would cost a great deal of money to conduct, it would be very difficult to carry out, or because it would take a very long time to get results.

When sociologists are conducting research, they need to consider some of the practical issues they may face. Questions that arise are:

How much will the research cost?

How long will it take to conduct the research?

How are they going to access participants?

Do they have the necessary equipment or training in order to complete their research?

Each research method has its own different practical considerations. Methods such as questionnaires will have issues over how to distribute questionnaires and how they will ensure enough people respond. While other methods such as observations will have different practical considerations, such as how long the sociologist would need to observe participants before they can gather enough information to draw a conclusion. The individual practical considerations for each method will be discussed in **section 2** and **section 3** of this workbook.

Ethical considerations

Ethical considerations refers to the way researchers plan their research to adhere to ethical guidelines about conducting research with human participants. Issues such as deception of participants, protecting participants and the researcher from psychological or physical harm, gaining informed consent, allowing participants the right to withdraw from the research and ensuring privacy and confidentiality are amongst these ethical considerations.

Before a sociologist can conduct their research, they need to submit their research proposal to an ethics committee. This is a board of sociologists that will examine the proposal and suggest any amendments to the research if they believe it to be in breach of the British Sociological Association's ethical guidelines. Researchers should consider:

- How they are going to gain informed consent for their research
- Whether the research will cause those being researched any physical or psychological harm
- How they are going to protect the confidentiality of the research participants

Some methods of research may breach one or more of these guidelines. It is up to the ethics committee to decide whether these breaches are necessary in order to obtain results.

Ethics in research is covered in more detail in **section 7** of this booklet.

Interpreting Results

Once a sociologist has conducted their research, they need to interpret the data that they have discovered. Their interpretation depends on different factors.

What method have they used?

What type of data have they collected?

Quantitative data is easier to interpret as it is in a numerical format. This enables the sociologist to present the data in several different formats, such as through bar charts, histograms, scatter-graphs, table and line graphs.

Qualitative data on the other hand will require more time to interpret. Sociologists have to analyse transcripts of interviews, notes taken from observations, and quantify responses to open questions. Some sociologists use a method known as content analysis to identify categories of behaviour or common issues that have been raised by participants. This is one way in which qualitative data can be transformed into quantitative data.

Interpreting data is discussed in further detail in **section 5** of this workbook.

Reporting Conclusions

One of the final stages in the research process is reporting the conclusions of the research. Sociologists will write up their research in an academic paper. These papers will display the aims and hypothesis of the research and a brief summary of the findings in a short paragraph at the start of the research called an abstract. The purpose of the abstract is for other sociologists researching that topic to be able to see if it is worth reading the full research paper and whether it will help them to further their own research.

Sociologists may be asked to present their research at academic conferences, where they will discuss their research with others in that field of study.

Peer Review

A **peer review** is an evaluation of scientific, academic, or professional work by others working in the same field.

One final stage is the research process is for sociologists to submit their research for peer review. This is where other sociologists will examine the research methodology that the sociologist used, check for errors or anomalies in the research and consider the findings of the research against what is already known about the topic area. This helps to improve both the reliability and validity of a sociologist's findings. Peer review is an important stage in making sure that the research is going to further our understanding of the social world.

KNOWLEDGE CHECK

1 In the table below arrange the following stages of the research process into chronological order:

peer review, pilot study, forming hypotheses, identifying a problem, conducting research, interpreting results, finding a sample, select a research method, reporting conclusions

2   Identify and describe one example of how sociologists select a sample for their research.   (3 marks)

_____

_____

_____

_____

_____

_____

_____

_____

3 Describe one reason why sociologists might conduct a pilot study.   (3 marks)

_____

_____

_____

_____

_____

_____

4 Describe one feature of sociological research that is seen as scientific.   (3 marks)

_____

_____

_____

_____

_____

_____

5 Identify and describe one example of the types of data that sociologists collect in their research.

(3 marks)

_____

_____

_____

_____

_____

_____

6 Which of the following is an example of qualitative data?   (1 mark)

a	Official statistics on criminal behaviour	☐
b	A personal account of poverty	☐
c	Wage gap percentage between males and females in society	☐
d	School league tables on student's achievement	☐

2 QUANTITATIVE AND QUALITATIVE METHODS

Surveys

A popular research method used by sociologists is surveys. The term survey refers to different types of method that look to measure the opinions, attitudes or behaviours of an individual at a specific moment in time. They come in a range of different formats. Questionnaires and structured interviews are both forms of survey, as they ask respondents for their opinions, preferences, behaviours and attitudes towards a certain topic.

These types of surveys usually generate quantitative data. This is because they use **closed questions** rather than **open questions**, and the answers can easily be quantified into numerical form. This is usually done by applying a code to each of the answers and giving each response a numerical value.

Closed questions

Closed questions are questions that have a fixed number of responses that have been decided by the researcher. Examples of the different types of closed question can be seen below:

Multiple choice

1   Which of the following is your favourite restaurant?

    a   McDonalds ☐

    b   Subway ☐

    c   KFC ☐

    d   Burger King ☐

Likert Scale

2   How likely are you to recommend McDonalds to a friend?

    a   Very likely ☐

    b   Somewhat likely ☐

    c   Neither likely nor unlikely ☐

    d   Somewhat unlikely ☐

    e   Very unlikely ☐

Yes/No response

3   Is this your first visit to McDonalds

    a   Yes ☐

    b   No ☐

While closed questions are very easy to answer and easy to quantify, there are issues with these questions. For example, in question 1, what if your favourite restaurant is not listed? This is referred to as the **imposition problem**. The researcher decides the responses a participant can give. This means that a participant's response may lack validity. Closed questions are also limited in that they do not allow the participant to expand on their answers, and so it may tell the research what the participants' attitude, opinion or preference is, but it does not explain why they feel this way.

Open Questions

An alternative form of questioning is open questions. Open questions have an infinite number of responses and are asked in such a way to get participants to expand on their answers. These questions will provide more information than closed questions as the participant is free to respond in whichever way they choose. Some examples of open questions are listed below.

1 **What is the difference in quality between McDonalds and Burger King?**

2 **Why do you think racism exists in society?**

3 **How does having a lack of money affect the choices you make?**

However, as responses are often less predictable and usually longer than the responses in closed questions, this causes problems for the researcher when they try to quantify the data. As a result, questionnaires and interviews with open questions tend to be more time consuming. Furthermore, they can lead to more misunderstandings between the researcher and the participant, as the researcher may interpret a response differently from the way the participant meant.

Extension Activity

Prepare a list of questions that you might use in an interview or on a questionnaire. The aim of the interview is to find out as much as you can about a friend's experience of education. Either choose to ask 10 closed or 6 open questions that you would ask a friend. Which do you think will be more likely for your friend to answer? Which do you think will be easiest to record responses from? Which one will take longer to draw conclusions from?

In practice, many questionnaires and interviews use a combination of both closed and open questions to try and get a more complete view of people's opinions, attitudes and preferences..

Attitude Surveys

A common type of survey is called an attitude survey. These measure the opinions and attitudes of people to social issues, such as voting intentions, attitudes to legal reforms, government spending, and educational standards. The example below is an attitude survey on confidence in policing.

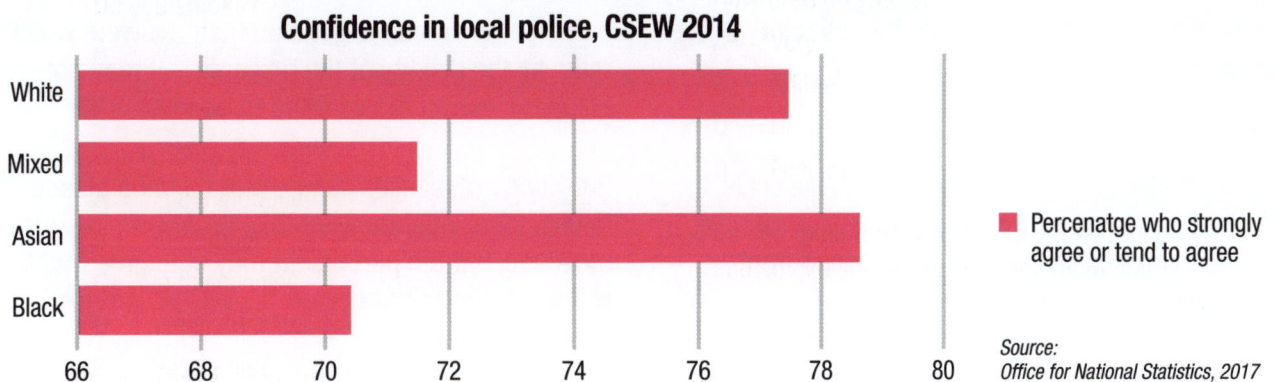

Confidence in local police, CSEW 2014

Group	Percentage who strongly agree or tend to agree
White	~77.5
Mixed	~71.5
Asian	~78.5
Black	~70.5

Source:
Office for National Statistics, 2017

In the bar chart above, which group has most confidence in their local police?

Which group has the least confidence in their local police?

What does the bar chart *not* tell you about the differences in confidence in local police?

Questionnaires

One of the most common types of survey are questionnaires. A questionnaire is a list of questions that are usually presented in a written format to respondents. They can be open (infinite responses), closed (finite responses) or mixed. Questionnaires can be administered via email, through the post, given to respondents to complete in their own time and return, or with a researcher present. The most famous questionnaire is the Census, a survey that is sent out to all households in the U.K. every ten years. This questionnaire collates data on the respondent's household, such as ages, religion, income, sexual orientation, disability, etc.

The use of questionnaires in sociological research has a range of strengths and limitations, and these depend upon the style of questions asked and the method of distribution.

Questionnaires with closed questions

These are questionnaires with a limited range of responses that the participant can give. The researcher will be able to pre-code the questions (give each responses a numerical score) and they provide quantitative data.

Strengths	Limitations
Easy to interpret, as the data collected is quantitative and will be in numerical form	Research imposes a range of responses on the participant. They are unable to choose freely
Collection of quantitative data means it is easy to see trends and patterns and can be presented in graphs	Potential for leading questions – ones that direct the participant towards an answer
Easily replicated which improves the **reliability** of the research	Participants cannot expand on their answers which reduces the validity of the research – it may not measure what it is supposed to be measuring
Can be produced and distributed on a large scale, which allows the researcher to gain a large sample, making the research generalisable to the target population	Pre-coded responses can be argued to be biased. Researchers will rate what they think is an important response, but the participant may not agree that it is the most important
Can be more cost-effective than other methods as they are cheaper to produce and less time-consuming to analyse	Lack of interaction with the researcher means it is difficult to pick up on cues that might suggest the participant is not telling the truth
Might give more honest answers as the absence of a researcher and anonymity means they do not have to give socially-desirable answers	Lower response rates for questionnaires as people do not see them as important. Those who do return questionnaires might have an interest in the research, giving biased answers

Reliability is a term used in research methods to explain whether a piece of research can be repeated with different participants and gain a similar result.

Questionnaires with open questions

Strengths	Limitations
Allows the participant to expand on their answers which will increases the validity of the research	More difficult to measure longer written responses which means that they can be time-consuming to analyse
Can be produced and distributed on a large scale, which allows the researcher to gain a large sample, making the research generalisable to the target population	Range of responses means that it may be difficult to replicate and achieve similar responses which reduces the reliability of the method
Can be more cost-effective than other methods as they are cheaper to produce	Having to provide written responses may mean that less people respond as they are more time-consuming to complete
Collect qualitative data that can give an insight into the meaning and motivations of people's actions	Harder to establish trends and patterns from qualitative data – could increase costs by having to train additional researchers to analyse written responses
People can respond fully and can highlight reasons the researcher may not have thought about previously. This could lead to them refining their research or conducting further research	Difficulties in extracting the meanings some people have. The researcher might mis-interpret what somebody means in their response and are unable to check if they are correct

Validity refers to whether the research really provides a true, accurate picture of what was set out to be discovered, including the meanings and motivations behind people's actions.

Distribution of Questionnaires

Questionnaires are often preferred by sociological researchers as they can be distributed widely using several different methods. The three most common methods are mailed, self-completion and face-to face. The strengths and limitations of these methods are discussed in the table below.

Distribution Method	Explanation	Strength	Limitation
Mailed	These questionnaires are sent to potential participants, either through the postal service or via email or by being directed to an online survey	Access to a large range of participants, particularly online questionnaires as they can reach an unlimited audience	Could be completed by others that do not fit the criteria for the research or are not part of the target population
Self-completion	These questionnaires are often handed to participants to complete and return in their own time	Easy to distribute and the researcher can explain the aims of the research	May not be returned and to gain a large sample would need additional help to administer which may be more costly
Face-to-face	These questionnaires are administered by a researcher who will ask the participant questions, in a similar way to a **structured interview**	Higher response rate with a researcher present	Interview effect. People could be more likely to give socially-desirable answers in the presence of a researcher

One of the key aspects of GCSE Sociology exams, is being able to identify the strengths and weakness of methods that have been used in key studies on the specification. Read the extract below, then complete the questions that follow.

CLASSIC TEXTS
PETER TOWNSEND
"POVERTY IN THE UNITED KINGDOM" 1979

" *Via the use of questionnaires, Peter Townsend developed a new way to measure poverty in the UK which he argued was more appropriate and useful than the official measures. Townsend was critical of the official state measurement of poverty. This was the sort of means-testing performed by government to determine that people were entitled to welfare support or benefits of various sorts. Townsend argued that the government of the day decided this measure based on their political views and how much money there was available to spend.*

Townsend developed a new measure instead which he described as relative deprivation. He accessed a large sample with his questionnaires and developed a measure - an index - based on a great number of things such as food, clothes, fuel, leisure activities, etc. He argued that people were relatively deprived if they did not have access to those things that were widely available in society. By this measure, far more people were relatively deprived than the state considered to be in poverty. He found that approximately 22% of the population was in poverty, compared with approximately 6% and 9% based on the other measures. "

(Extract taken from https://www.tutor2u.net/sociology/reference/classic-texts-peter-townsend-poverty-in-the-united-kingdom-1979)

What type of data did Townsend collect in his research? (1 mark)

Identify and describe one advantage of using this method to collect data into poverty in the UK. (4 marks)

Describe one disadvantage of using the method Townsend used. (3 marks)

Identify and describe one alternative method Townsend could have used to collect the required data on poverty. (4 marks)

Interviews

Another method that sociologists use to gain an insight into social issues are interviews. An interview is a conversation between a researcher and a respondent that can be either structured, semi-structed, unstructured or group interviews. In a structured interview, the research will have a specific list of questions to ask (known as an **interview schedule**) which they will ask the respondent in the same order. An unstructured interview will have a limited amount of pre-prepared questions for the researcher to ask, with further questions being added depending on the responses of the respondent. A semi-structured interview combines elements of both, with an interview schedule that is flexible and allows the researcher to probe further if necessary. A group interview, often referred to as a focus group, will ask questions of several participants at the same time and responses will be noted from those who make them.

Whilst each of these methods have their own strengths and limitations in collecting data, the role of the interviewer is one of the most important factors. An interviewer's level of skill, their appearance and perceived social class (and other social characteristics), and their ability to develop a rapport (connection) with those being interviewed may influence the responses that a participant gives. This is referred to as **interviewer bias**.

Structured interviews

Structured interviews take the form of a list of standardised questions (everybody who participates is asked the same questions in the same order). They have very similar characteristics to a face-to-face questionnaire and because of the rigid nature of the questions, interviewers do not need to be trained as thoroughly as if they were conducting an unstructured interview. Most structured interviews record quantitative data, which means they can be analysed easily.

The strengths and limitations of this method can be found in the chart below.

Strengths	Limitations
Having standardised questions means that other researchers can repeat this method easily, increasing reliability	The rigid nature of the questions means that if participants disclose something of interest that is not covered in the questions, the interviewer is unable to follow it up
Presence of an interviewer means that questions can be explained to participants, unlike in questionnaires	The presences of a researcher means that participants may lie and give socially desirable answers – the answers they think the interviewer wants to hear
The use of standardised questions means that interviewers require less training, reducing the costs of the research	Does not disclose meanings and motivations of people's behaviour as mostly gather quantitative data

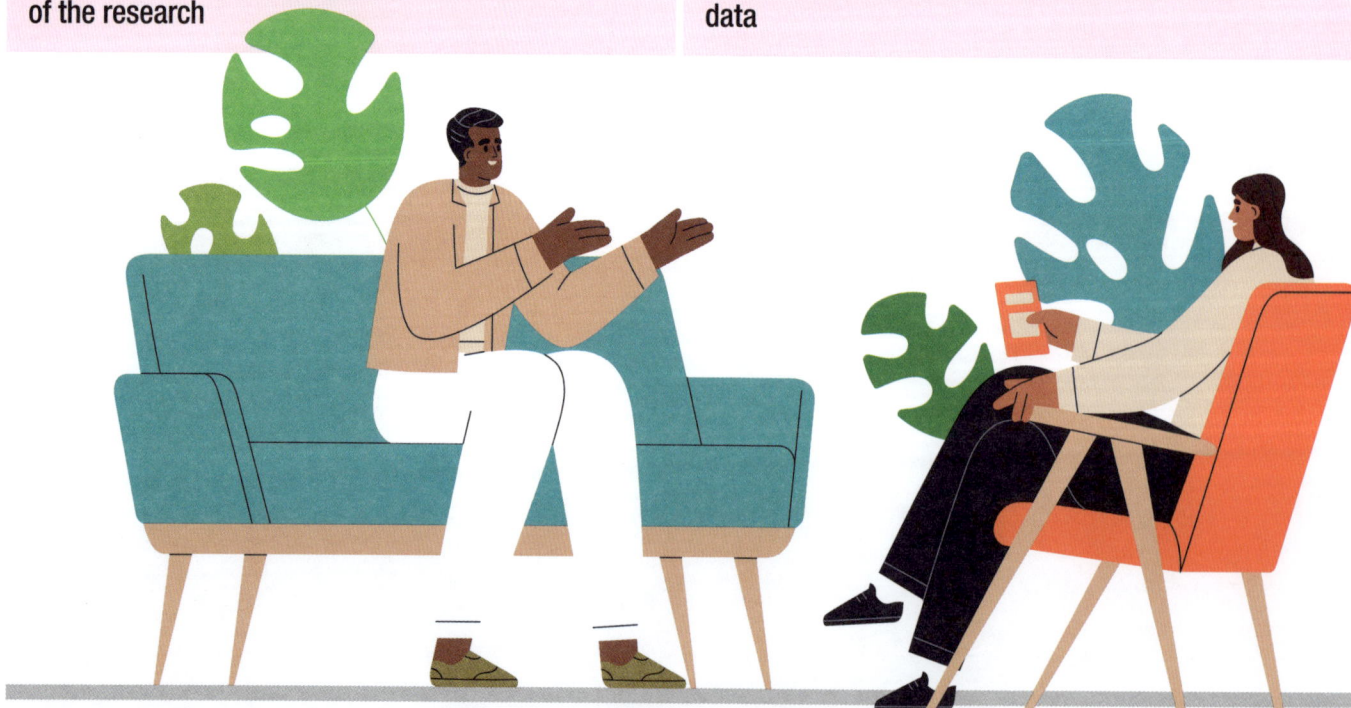

Unstructured interviews

Unstructured interviews take the form of a guided conversation, with the interviewer having themes and topics that they may want to discuss with the participant, but no set structure. This enables the researcher to ask follow-up questions to the participant if they disclose something that is relevant to their research that they may not have considered. Unstructured interviews obtain qualitative data which provides the researcher with a good insight into the participant's experiences.

The strengths and limitations of this method can be found in the chart below.

Strengths	Limitations
Gathers qualitative data which allows the interviewer to understand the meaning and motivations behind people's actions	Can go off topic and not remain focused on the aims of the research
Can reveal ideas and viewpoints that the researcher may not have thought of, and these can be explored using follow-up questions	Unstructured interviews are not standardised and so it will be difficult to repeat an interview and gain similar results – lacks reliability
Greater flexibility allows researchers to develop a rapport with respondents and make judgements about whether the questions are distressing for the participant	More time-consuming to analyse transcripts of the interviews, which leads to fewer interviews taking place and a smaller sample of data collected
Can obtain more valid data as the interviewer can guide the conversation and ensure that they obtain information that fits in with the aims of the research	Participants may give responses that they think the researcher wants to hear. Interviewer bias may be increased by developing a rapport with participants
Interviewer can observe non-verbal cues (body language, etc.) of the participant to judge whether they are telling the truth	Interviewer requires more training in order to conduct the interview, and this may make the research more costly

Semi-structured interviews

Semi-structured interviews are a compromise between unstructured and structured interviews. Whilst they may have an interview schedule, the interviewer is free to follow-up on the responses that participants have given. These types of interview can provide both quantitative and qualitative data, which allows the research to have greater validity than a structured interview and more reliability than an unstructured interview.

Group interviews (focus groups)

A final form of interview is a group interview or focus group. It can take the form of a structured, semi-structured and unstructured interview and is seen as being a good way of obtaining large amounts of data in a short space of time. These are often used by businesses when launching a new product as it gives the researcher an opportunity to gather a lot of information from a variety of people. One advantage of group interviews is that responses from participants might prompt others into disclosing their own views, ideas and opinions. However, when dealing with sensitive topics, people may be less likely to disclose information in front of others. Another issue with group interviews is that one or two people may dominate the discussion, and not all opinions or views are heard. Some people may have conflicting views with others and express a different opinion than the one they really hold in order to fit in with the rest of the group, reducing the validity of the research.

One of the key aspects of GCSE Sociology exams, is being able to identify the strengths and weakness of methods that have been used in key studies on the specification. Read the extract below, then complete the questions that follow.

PAT CARLEN
"WOMEN, CRIME & POVERTY" 1988

> *This feminist study, based on unstructured interviews with 39 women, looks at why some women commit crimes.*
>
> *Most sociologists who have considered the issue of gender and crime have focused on why women commit far fewer crimes than men - after all, that is what the crime statistics show us. However, some women do commit crimes, and Carlen examined that question. She concluded that working-class women made a class deal and a gender deal that generally kept them under control. The class deal was that they would work hard in exchange for pay which they could then use to pay for consumer goods. The gender deal was that they should do domestic labour and give love and companionship to their husbands, in exchange for love and financial support. Both these deals keep working-class women respectable.*
>
> *It was, Carlen suggested, when these deals broke down that working-class women were then more likely to commit crimes, as a rational choice.*
>
> *For Carlen both these "deals" were exploitative. As a feminist she believed that women were exploited in families, and she also believed that the working class was exploited by employers in the capitalist system (agreeing with Marxists). However, there was an illusion of fairness and respectability about these deals that, most of the time, kept women under control.*

(Extract taken from https://www.tutor2u.net/sociology/reference/classic-texts-pat-carlen-women-crime-poverty-1988)

Identify and describe the method used in Carlen's research, including what you know of her perspective on female criminality. (4 marks)

Identify and describe one disadvantage of using unstructured interviews to conduct Carlen's research. (4 marks)

Describe one alternative method that could have been used to obtain data on reasons why women commit fewer crimes than men. (4 marks)

Identify and describe one advantage of using unstructured interviews to investigate people's motivations for committing crime. (4 marks)

Observations

An observation is a research method where a researcher observes the behaviour of a group or an individual in order to witness social behaviours. These can be either participant or non-participant. Additionally, each of these types can be overt (where subjects are aware that they are being watched) or covert (where they are unaware). Observations are usually associated with a methodological approach called ethnography.

Ethnography is a research methodology that is a systematic examination of a cultural phenomenon whereby the researcher studies the group by viewing society through their point of view. This method is often very high in validity as it enables the researcher to experience what the subjects of their research would experience.

Observation can be conducted in a structured way, following an observation schedule which sets out time periods and behaviours to monitor, or an unstructured way, noting down observations as they occur.

Non-participant observations

A non-participant observation is an observation whereby the researcher observes from a distance and does not take part in the activities of the group. Non-participant observations allow researchers to see the interactions between group members without having the ability to influence their behaviour. This method could gather both quantitative data (if a researcher records categories of behaviour) or qualitative data (if they record all behaviours and analyse these individually).

The strengths and limitations of this method are listed below.

Strengths	Limitations
Observer is detached from the actions of the participants so is less likely to influence the result	If those being observed are aware of the observer's presence, they may alter their behaviour. This is known as the **Hawthorne Effect**
If the researcher is not participating in the activities, they are more likely to be able to observe the behaviour of others without having to gain consent. This means participants are less likely to change their behaviour	Keeping a distance from the participants might run a greater risk of misunderstanding actions. If the research is covert, the researcher will not be able to ask for clarification
Structured non-participant observations can produce quantitative data which can be checked by another observer who is observing at the same time – this increases reliability	Non-participant observation could be costly and time-consuming if other researchers need to be trained to observe certain behaviours
Can use recording equipment to observe and show to another researcher to check findings	Does not explain the meaning and motivations of those being observed, merely tells us how they behave in a particular context

Participant observations

A participant observation is a research method where the researcher is directly involved in the activities of the group and could potentially influence their actions. Whilst this is seen as having greater validity, it could also lead to the research becoming biased in favour of the researcher's hypothesis. Participant observations can either be overt or covert. It tends to produce qualitative data. Being involved in the activities of the group gives the researcher a better idea of the experiences of the group as they are involved in the activities themselves. This generates greater understanding of their worldview and helps the researcher to develop empathy with their research subjects.

The strengths and limitations of this method are listed below.

Strengths	Limitations
Directly involved in the action so can collect lots of qualitative data at first hand	Behaviour of those being observed may alter if they are aware that they are being observed
The nature of participant observation means that, as the researcher continues their research, new ideas and concepts may occur which will inform their research	Some groups are difficult to gain access to, particularly if illegal or immoral behaviour is involved

People are studied in their natural environment which means they may act more naturally than if in a false environment such as a laboratory	To continue observing a group or individuals can be costly and time-consuming as the research may take a long period of time to complete
Gain in-depth understanding of the experiences of the group through observing and taking part in their day-to-day activities	Due to cost and time taken, samples are going to be small and therefore difficult to generalise

Covert observations

An important factor that influences the strengths and limitations of research is whether it is conducted without the knowledge of those being observed. Covert observations may be able to generate a lot of valid data, as participants act more naturally when they are being observed, but there are several other practical and ethical limitations that arise from using a covert style of observation.

Practical issues with covert observations include:

- Gaining access to the group. Researchers may have to spend time and money establishing a cover in order to be able to research groups without their knowledge.
- Maintaining that cover. It would be difficult to write notes or use recording equipment when in the presence of those being observed as it would arouse suspicion and put the research at risk.
- Leaving the research. As the researcher will have established connections with the group, disappearing from the group being observed will be difficult to do.

Ethical issues with covert observations include:

- Deceiving participants. As a cover is established, the researcher is not being honest with those being researched. Furthermore, they are unaware they are part of a sociological study, which is unethical.
- Protection from harm. Many covert observations are carried out on illegal or immoral activities and could involve the researcher putting themselves in danger. Furthermore, they may also witness others in danger and ethically should try to prevent this. However, if they do, they risk exposing themselves as researchers, which could put themselves at further risk.
- Confidentiality. Researchers will have to maintain the confidentiality of individuals in their research, and this could pose moral and ethical issues for researchers if they were made aware of crimes committed by those that they are observing. Should they inform the authorities if they know crimes have been committed? If so, what level of criminal behaviour would they report?

Extension Activity

Some of the most famous sociological studies have been observations and these have been groundbreaking in developing our understanding of hard-to-reach groups in society. From the list below, research one observation and note the problems that the sociologists had when conducting the research.

James Patrick – A Glasgow Gang Observed

Laud Humphries – Tearoom Trade

Geoff Pearson – The Researcher as Hooligan

John Griffin – Black Like Me

Mixed methods approaches

Some sociologists choose to use a mixed methods approach to studying society. This is when a researcher will choose both quantitative and qualitative research methods to investigate a social issue. Initially, they may use a quantitative method, such as closed questionnaires to see patterns and trends in research and then highlight some of those patterns and trends and focus on some of the more common problems. Then, they may use a qualitative method, such as unstructured interviews with some of the participants, or others with similar experiences, to try and obtain an understanding of the motivations behind behaviour highlighted in the first part of their research. The use of two different methods is often referred to as triangulation.

However, not all researchers choose to select quantitative and qualitative methods to conduct their research. One of the key texts on the AQA GCSE Sociology specification is a study conducted by Paul Willis. Willis used a range of mostly qualitative methods in his research as he attempted to gain a greater understanding of the behaviours of young boys from a school in the Midlands. An excerpt from the study is presented below. Read the excerpt and answer the questions that follow.

CLASSIC TEXTS
PAUL WILLIS
"LEARNING TO LABOUR" 1977

Paul Willis used a wide range of research methods - including observations and interviews - to really try and see education from the children's point of view. As a Marxist, he was interested in conflict in education and why working-class children went on to do working-class jobs. But he reached quite different conclusions from Bowles & Gintis.

Willis' study of working-class boys in a Midlands school has become a classic. His study focused on "the lads" - a group of working-class boys who were disruptive, misbehaved and had a very negative attitude to education. They had formed what Willis called an anti-school subculture. Within this subculture it was "cool" to "mess about" and to fail. It really turned the values of the school on their head. From the perspective of this subculture, children who the school viewed positively were the "ear'oles" ("swots"). The last thing you wanted was praise from a teacher. Instead, children could get praise within the group for truancy, bad behaviour and discriminatory attitudes (there was a lot of racism, sexism and homophobia within the group).

*Willis used a wide range of research methods to try and get as true a picture as possible. However, it has been suggested that the boys may have acted up more to "show off" to Willis. This might have occurred when they were being observed (the **Hawthorne Effect** - people behave differently when they know they're being watched) and when they were interviewed (an **interviewer effect**).*

(Extract taken from https://www.tutor2u.net/sociology/reference/classic-texts-paul-willis-learning-to-labour-1977)

Identify and describe one research method used by Willis in his research, including what you know of his perspective on anti-school subcultures in education. (4 marks)

Identify and describe one advantage of using overt observations in sociological research. (4 marks)

KNOWLEDGE CHECK

In the following activity, you need to highlight all research methods that fit the criteria given.

Has high reliability

Overt participant observation	Structured interview	Unstructured interview	Closed questionnaire
Open questionnaire	Semi-structured interview	Covert participant observation	Overt non-participant observation

Has a researcher present

Overt participant observation	Structured interview	Unstructured interview	Closed questionnaire
Open questionnaire	Semi-structured interview	Covert participant observation	Overt non-participant observation

Produces qualitative data

Overt participant observation	Structured interview	Unstructured interview	Closed questionnaire
Open questionnaire	Semi-structured interview	Covert participant observation	Overt non-participant observation

Has high validity

Overt participant observation	Structured interview	Unstructured interview	Closed questionnaire
Open questionnaire	Semi-structured interview	Covert participant observation	Overt non-participant observation

Is preferred by ethnographers

Overt participant observation	Structured interview	Unstructured interview	Closed questionnaire
Open questionnaire	Semi-structured interview	Covert participant observation	Overt non-participant observation

Fill in the blanks on the following paragraphs using the key terms below:

Some sociologists adopt a _____ approach to research. This is where two or more research methods are used to conduct the research. This is performed so that researchers can improve the _____ and _____ of their research by combining _____ data and _____ data. This process is also known as _____.

_____ can either be participant or non-participant. In a _____ _____ the researcher is not involved in the activities of the group and observes from a distance. In a _____ _____, the researcher is actively involved in the day-to-day activities of the group and gains an insight into subjects' real-life experiences. This results in the research having more validity. Furthermore, the research can be conducted in a _____ or _____ manner, but choosing the former has some _____ issues.

_____ have an _____ which is a list of questions that are asked in a set order to each of the participants. This means that the research can easily be _____. Furthermore, the standardised nature means it can be widely distributed and a large _____ collected, making the research more generalisable. Alternatively _____ may have a list of topics or themes that the researcher would like to cover but there are no set _____. This means that the researcher can _____ for more information. Consequently, only a _____ amount of participants can take part.

Missing terms

Validity	Reliability	Limited	Unstructured interview	Participant observation
Triangulation	Questions	Interview schedule	Sample	Structured Interviews
Non-participant	Quantitative	Qualitative	Mixed Methods	Observations
Replicated	Probe	Covert	Overt	Ethical

3 TYPES OF DATA

A sociologist's choice of method is often decided by the types of data they require for their research. As we have seen in section 2, different types of questionnaire, interview and observation produce different types of data. This is summarised in the table below:

Quantitative data	Qualitative data
Questionnaires with closed questions	Questionnaires with open questions
Structured interviews	Unstructured interviews
Non-participant observations with structured observation schedule	Participant observations

While the type of data required may influence a researcher's decision, it is important to be able to analyse the strengths and limitations of both, and why the researcher would look to produce that type of data in the first place.

What influences a researcher's choice of data?

A researcher's choice of data is influenced by several factors: their methodological preference, their values, the aims of their research and what they plan to do with the research.

Methodological Preference

Sociologists have preferences for the way they conduct research that is based upon their own view of how society works. Some sociologists view society as being influenced by structural forces and that these forces shape the behaviour of individuals. These sociologists prefer positivist methodologies. Positivism suggests that society shapes the behaviour of humans and that human beings can be studied in a scientific way. The use of the scientific methods in research means that positivist sociologists aim to obtain quantitative data.

Structural theories believe that:

- Society is more important than the individual and continues long after individuals have left the society
- The social institutions, such as education, media, family and religion shape our behaviour
- Social processes such as socialisation, are conducted by these institutions for individuals to behave in a certain manner
- Human beings are predictable and will behave in similar ways when social forces act upon them

Positivism is the view that sociology should use similar research methods to the natural sciences (Chemistry, Biology, Physics) in order to understand the behaviour of human beings in society. They prefer the use of quantitative data in their research.

A further feature of research methods that positivist sociologists look for that makes research more scientific is reliability.

What do sociologists mean by reliability?

Other sociologists would suggest that society is made up of individual actors and that human beings demonstrate free will and that their behaviour is not predictable or formulaic. Social action theorists prefer **interpretivist** methods. **Interpretivists** are more concerned with the actions and experiences of individuals in society. Their focus is on trying to understand how humans think, reflect and act in society. They argue that humans make conscious decisions and are independent. For this reason, they prefer qualitative data in their research.

Social action theories believe that:
- Individuals make conscious decisions to behave – they have free will
- Social institutions and processes are not fixed and are constructed by individuals and therefore individuals dictate social norms
- Individuals have different experiences and it is these experiences and interactions with other individuals that shape their behaviour
- Suggest that sociologists should look at the individual rather than society as a whole

Interpretivism is the view that in order to understand human experiences we must understand the meanings and motivations behind an individual's actions. They suggest sociology should not employ scientific methods to understand humans, rather look for 'verstehen' or empathy with their subjects.

Interpretivists look for their research to have greater validity.

What do sociologists mean by validity?

Values in Sociology

Another influence in a sociologist's choice of method is values. Values are what sociologists hold to be important when conducting research. Positivist sociologists believe that researchers should put their values to one side (sociology should be value-free) and that the sociologist should research society without bias, using scientific methods. Positivists believe quantitative data is **objective** (**value-free**) as it is factual data, rather than being based upon opinions. Interpretivists, on the other hand, suggest that values are important when conducting research. They prefer methods that rely upon **subjective** judgements (based upon opinion or an individual's values). These are methods that produce qualitative data.

Aims of the Research

The choice of using quantitative or qualitative data often depends upon the aims of the research. Large-scale research, such as examining patterns and trends in educational achievement would be better suited to quantitative data. This is because the researcher is looking for a method that allows them to easily compare students from one social group (social class, gender or ethnicity) against another.

In contrast, if a researcher's aim is to understand the motivations behind people's actions, they are more likely to choose qualitative research, which allows them to develop a greater understanding of individuals and groups. Methods such as unstructured interviews and participant observations will give researchers more insight into the motivations of people. For example, research by Willis and Carlen focused on understanding why boys were more likely to form anti-school subcultures and women less likely to break the law. These aims could not have been achieved through examining quantitative data.

In the table below, suggest whether the social issues would be better investigated using quantitative or qualitative methods:

Issue	Quantitative or Qualitative?
Examining the number of people in the UK below the poverty line	
Examining the experiences of women who have been victims of domestic violence	
Examining the experience of children who have been bullied at school	
Examining the differences in criminality between ethnic groups	
Examining the experiences of migrant workers in the UK post-Brexit	
Examining social class differences in life expectancy	

Intention of the Research

A further consideration when choosing whether to use quantitative or qualitative data is what the researcher intends to use the data for. Many researchers conduct their work on behalf of governments and businesses, who are looking to establish trends and patterns of behaviour in order to plan for social spending or deciding on their target market for new products. This type of research is more likely to use quantitative data due to its larger sample size. The same can be said for charities, who may use quantitative data to demonstrate emerging social issues, such as child poverty or homelessness. They may also use this data to plan where to allocate resources to help as many people as they can. Other sociologists will conduct research with the intention of widening the knowledge base of a certain topic. Often these are funded by universities. In contemporary society, sociological research has focused largely on the experiences of individuals, particularly those that have little access to power. These sociologists would prefer to use qualitative data to challenge stereotypes and allow the voices of the 'underdog' to be heard.

Other research methods that produce quantitative or qualitative data

So far, we have examined the strengths and limitations of the most common sociological research methods: questionnaires, interviews and observations. These can produce either quantitative or qualitative research methods based upon their structure. However, there are other methods that sociologists use which usually produce either quantitative or qualitative data.

Quantitative Research

Two other methods that produce quantitative data that are used by sociologists are experiments and statistics – both official and non-official.

Experiments

Experiments are not a common research method in sociology as it is very difficult to control variables. The idea of an experiment is that – whether in a laboratory or in the field – phenomena are observed in a tightly-controlled environment, to see the impact of certain variables. There are different types of experiments that sociologists might use, however many of the examples of experiments in sociology come from other social science disciplines, such as psychology.

Laboratory or Controlled Experiments

Experiments look for the effect that manipulated variables (**independent variables, or IVs**) have on measured variables (**dependent variables**, or DVs), i.e. causal effects.

Laboratory experiments pay attention to eliminating the effects of other, **extraneous variables**, by controlling them (i.e. removing or keeping them constant) in an artificial environment. This makes it more likely for researchers to find a causal effect, having confidence that no variables other than changes in an IV can affect a resulting DV. Laboratory experiments are the most heavily controlled form of experimental research.

One of the most famous laboratory experiments that has been used in sociology is Bandura's Bobo Doll experiment to demonstrate the impact of the media on its audience. Some of the strengths and weaknesses of laboratory experiments are listed below.

Strengths	Limitations
High control over extraneous variables means cause and effect can be established	Data collected may lack ecological validity, as the artificial nature of laboratory experiments can cast doubt over whether the results reflect the nature of real-life scenarios
Results of laboratory experiments tend to be reliable, as the conditions created (and thus results produced) can be replicated	There is a high risk of the Hawthorne Effect, i.e. participants may alter their behaviour based on their interpretation of the purpose of the experiment.
Variables can be measured accurately with the tools made available in a laboratory setting, which may otherwise be impossible for experiments conducted 'in the field'	There is also a risk of experimenter bias, e.g. researchers' expectations may affect how they interact with participants (affecting participants' behaviour) or alter their interpretation of the results

Field Experiments

Field experiments are conducted in a natural setting (e.g. at a sports event or on public transport), as opposed to the artificial environment created in laboratory experiments. Some variables cannot be controlled due to the unpredictability of these real-life settings (e.g. the public interacting with participants), but an independent variable will still be altered for a dependent variable to be measured against.

One of the most famous field experiments used in sociology is Rosenthal and Jacobsen's *'Pygmalion in the classroom'* which looked at the effects of teacher interactions on students that had been labelled as high achievers. Some of the strengths and limitations of field experiments are in the table below.

Strengths	Limitations
Field experiments generally yield results with higher ecological validity than laboratory experiments, as the natural settings will relate to real life	Extraneous variables could confound results due to the reduced control experimenters have over them in non-artificial environments, which makes it difficult to find truly causal effects between independent and dependent variables
The Hawthorne Effect is less of an issue with field experiments than laboratory experiments (i.e. participants are less likely to adjust their natural behaviour according to their interpretation of the study's purpose, as they might not know they are in a study)	Ethical principles must be considered, such as the lack of informed consent; if participants are not made aware of their participation in an experiment, privacy must be respected during observations and participants must be debriefed appropriately when observations come to an end
	Precise replication of the natural environment of field experiments is understandably difficult, so they have poor reliability, unlike laboratory experiments where the exact conditions can be recreated

Both types of experiments are scientific and produce qualitative data. However, they are smaller in scale than some other methods due to the cost of equipment and the time taken to conduct the experiments.

Official Statistics

Official statistics are a source of quantitative data. The term refers to any set of data collected by the government or other official body, for example official crime statistics, unemployment figures, demographic statistics collected from the census, etc.

Statistics are usually compiled through alternative methods such as questionnaires, like the census. They are also collated through social institutions, such as the education system, the police and the civil service records. For example, each year schools report the results of their examinations to the government and they publish these in league tables. The police submit records of crimes committed to the Home Office and these statistics are published also, while businesses and individuals report the amount of money they earn to HMRC which then reports on average incomes in the UK. Other institutions, such as the Department for Work and Pensions will record the number of people receiving benefits or registered as looking for work. The Department for Health will also publish data on the number of hospital admissions, waiting times for treatment and the number of cases of specific illnesses.

The advantage of this type of quantitative data is that it gives users a view of social issues across the country. For governments, it allows them to plan budgets and see where action is needed to make sure society runs correctly. However, some would suggest that these figures can be manipulated to serve political purposes. Definitions of criminal activity can change, the amount people need to earn to be classed as living in poverty can be adjusted and unemployment figures can be altered to only show those people without any work, rather than those who are working less hours than they need to survive. This is referred to as **selective use of data**.

Official statistics are reported by the Office for National Statistics and are readily available to the public and to sociological researchers once they have been published.

Non-official Statistics

Non-official statistics are another quantitative source of data that is available, however they have not been collected by official government agencies. Charities often supply these forms of data, such as the Joseph Rowntree Foundation which produces data on the number of people living in poverty. Another charity that produces non-official statistics is the Trussell Trust, which reports on the number of people using foodbanks, another indicator of poverty.

As these statistics are not collated by official government institutions, some sociologists would argue that they are not as reliable as official statistics and do not come under as much scrutiny. Furthermore, some of the figures obtained are estimates and their definitions of poverty do not exactly match those of the government. However, it can be argued that charities are less likely to be politically-motivated and therefore their reporting of data is more objective and more accurate.

Qualitative Research

Qualitative data is produced by unstructured interviews, open-ended questionnaires and participant observations. However, there are other research methods that produce qualitative data and are used by sociologists to investigate society. Two such methods are case studies and longitudinal studies.

Case Studies

Case studies are very detailed investigations of an individual or small group of people, usually regarding an unusual social phenomenon of interest to a researcher. Due to a small sample, the case study can conduct an in-depth analysis of the individual/group.

Strengths	Limitations
Case studies create opportunities for a rich yield of data, and the depth of analysis can in turn bring high levels of validity	There is little control over several variables involved in a case study, so it is difficult to confidently establish any causal relationships between variables
The detail collected on a single case may lead to interesting findings that conflict with current theories and stimulate new paths for research	Case studies are unusual by nature, so will have poor reliability as replicating them exactly will be unlikely
Case studies are part of a mixed methods approach that can be flexible to adapt to the social context of those being studied	Due to being very small-scale there is a limited possibility of the data being able to be generalised to others

The in-depth nature of case studies means that they are used quite rarely in sociology, but when they are used they can provide researchers with a valuable insight into the workings, meaning and motivations behind a person or group's behaviour.

An example of a case study is Paul Willis' 'Learning to Labour' which involved an in-depth study of a group of male students from a school in Wolverhampton. Another is Heelas and Woodhead's case study of spirituality in Kendal (the Kendal Project).

Longitudinal Studies

Another method that produces qualitative data is a longitudinal study. This type of research method looks at a group of individuals over a long period of time, repeating observations or interviews at frequent intervals. There are three different types of longitudinal study: panel studies, cohort studies and retrospective studies. Some longitudinal studies focus on quantitative data, such as employment status, income, family type, health and relationship status and compare large amounts of data and attempt to draw conclusions from these. Qualitative longitudinal studies are more likely to be focused on smaller cohorts, with individuals having one or more shared characteristics and being interviewed at specific intervals of time.

An example of a qualitative longitudinal study is the Granada TV programme Seven Up! which followed the lives of a group of children who turned 7 in the same year and returned to interview them at 7-year intervals (14, 21, 28, etc.)

Strengths	Limitations
In depth studies that provide large amounts of data	People may drop out of the research – this is called the attrition rate
Can demonstrate changes over lifetimes, such as attitude changes and social mobility	Take a long period of time to complete and therefore researchers will wait a long time for the results of research to be found
They can examine the impact of life events on individuals over a period, rather than providing a snapshot of issues, such as poverty or racism	Difficult for the sample to be representative of general population due to the small size of the research.

Some universities and governments have funded cohort and panel longitudinal studies that continue to run, but their limited size means that often the findings of such research are not adapted into policies and practices in wider society.

Choosing quantitative or qualitative data?

The following chart compares the advantages of quantitative versus qualitative data in research. Highlight which is the correct characteristic of that type of data in the first 6 boxes and give examples of research methods that produce that type of data in the final box.

Quantitative Data	Qualitative Data
Preferred by positivists or interpretivists?	Preferred by positivists or Interpretivists?
Scientific method? Yes/no	Scientific method? Yes/no
Structural or social action?	Structural or social action?
Objective or subjective?	Objective or subjective?
Large scale or small scale?	Large scale or small scale?
Reliability or validity?	Reliability or validity?
Examples of methods:	Examples of methods:

KNOWLEDGE CHECK

1 Which of the following methods produces qualitative data? (1 mark)

    a   Unstructured interviews ☐

    b   Structured interviews ☐

    c   Closed questionnaires ☐

    d   Official statistics ☐

2 Identify and describe one advantage of using qualitative methods when researching anti-school sub-cultures. (4 marks)

_____

_____

_____

_____

_____

_____

_____

_____

_____

_____

_____

3 Identify and explain one disadvantage of using mailed questionnaires with students with low levels of literacy. (3 marks)

_____

_____

_____

_____

_____

_____

_____

_____

4   Describe one method of obtaining quantitative data on the different types of family in society.   (3 marks)

_____

_____

_____

_____

_____

_____

5   Identify and describe one advantage of using victim questionnaires, such as the Crime Survey of England and Wales, to measure the level of crime in society.   (4 marks)

_____

_____

_____

_____

_____

_____

_____

_____

6   Identify and describe one disadvantage of using questionnaires to assess the differences in life chances of different social groups.   (4 marks)

_____

_____

_____

_____

_____

_____

_____

_____

Primary sources of data

Primary data refers to data that has been collected first hand by a researcher. By using primary data, the researcher can be more certain that the data they generate fits the criteria for their research. These sources can produce quantitative or qualitative data.

In the boxes below, give examples of primary data that you have already studied in this book.

Primary sources that produce quantitative data	Primary sources that produce qualitative data

Advantages of using primary sources

- Researcher has designed the questions, observations and definitions of social issues to fit in with their research, which gives it a greater chance of validity.
- Following a more scientific research method enables the researcher to have their research replicated, improving the reliability of the research.

Disadvantages of using primary sources

- Some research can be costly and time-consuming for the researcher to conduct.
- Researcher may have difficulties accessing groups because of personal characteristics or geographical constraints.

Secondary sources of data

Secondary data is data that has already been collected for another purpose. Secondary data can be quantitative, such as official statistics, or qualitative, such as newspaper articles, journals, historical documents or diaries.

Official statistics has been covered in section 3 of this workbook. The other secondary sources it is worth examining are: historical documents, personal documents, and media sources.

Historical documents

These can include parish records of families, official government documents from a previous era, raw census data and minutes of meetings from companies and organisations. They help researchers to understanding events from the past that otherwise they may not be able to study. They provide a useful insight into the reactions of people to social events and ways in which society was structured in the past. However, they can be misinterpreted because of changes in language, hard to access due to legislation and cost, and may only represent a viewpoint of one person, which sociologists cannot be sure is valid.

Personal documents

These are documents such as letters and diaries that have been kept by individuals that provide an insight into the thoughts and feelings of people. Letters, such as those sent home by Polish migrants to America in the 1920s (Thomas and Znaniecki's research) may be the only insight that sociologists have into social events. However, they may lack credibility or not reflect the general feelings of the time as they are one person's thoughts and feelings. They may also be hard to access due to being part of a family's history.

Media sources

Media sources, such as newspaper articles, TV programmes, films and documentaries are a useful secondary source of qualitative data. They can provide an insight into the times or show how popular culture has represented a certain group or individual. Many sociologists who study media use content analysis to convert qualitative data into quantitative data, for example counting the amount of times women speak in mainstream films and programmes (Bechdel Test). However, a disadvantage of using these sources is that they often only represent the views of the editor or director and do not represent the views of the audience.

Content analysis is a research method that aims to turn qualitative data into quantitative data by categorising the content of articles, films, documents and other secondary sources into easily identifiable themes. The frequency of these themes in secondary sources is then counted and conclusions drawn from the quantitative data.

KNOWLEDGE CHECK

1   Which of the following is a secondary qualitative source   (1 mark)

    a   Historical documents   ☐

    b   Official statistics   ☐

    c   Non-official statistics   ☐

    d   Non-participant observation   ☐

2   Identify and describe one advantage of using secondary sources to investigate changes
in women's role in society.   (4 marks)

_____

_____

_____

_____

_____

_____

_____

_____

_____

_____

_____

3   Describe one reason why sociologists might not use official statistics
in their research.   (3 marks)

_____

_____

_____

_____

_____

_____

4   Identify and explain one disadvantage of using a longitudinal study to research educational achievement in schools.   (4 marks)

_____

_____

_____

_____

_____

_____

_____

_____

_____

5   Identify one method used in the measurement of crime and describe one advantage of using this method.   (4 marks)

_____

_____

_____

_____

_____

_____

_____

_____

_____

Sociologists need to be able to analyse and interpret data that is presented to them to find patterns and trends in their research. In this section of this book, you will be presented with data in different formats and will be asked to examine the patterns and trends within the data. This is known as data analysis. Most of the data on these pages is taken from research that ties in with some of the main learning aims of GCSE Sociology. In the exams, you will be presented with similar data, some from the key texts, and others from other sociological studies.

Data analysis is the process of understanding the trends and patterns present in data through a systematic examination of the available data.

Families and Households

Ethnicity	Cohabiting %	Lone Parent %	Married or same-sex civil partners %	One person %	Other %	Pensioner couple %
Asian	3.5	8.8	47	17	21.7	2.1
Black	6.8	24.3	21.6	31.7	14.1	1.5
Mixed	11.2	19.1	19.9	35.2	12.9	1.7
White	10.3	10.2	32.9	30.9	6.8	8.9
Other	5.2	10.5	37	30.7	15	1.4

Source: UK Census 2011

In the table above, identify:

1 **The percentage of black one person households**

2 **The percentage of white married or same-sex civil partners**

3 **The most common household type for Asians**

4 **The least common household type for mixed ethnicity groups**

5 **The percentage of white lone parent households**

6 **The percentage of Asian pensioner couples**

7 **The percentage of other ethnicity cohabiting couples**

8 **The ethnic group with the highest percentage of one person households**

Percentage of people within each white ethnic group that fall into each age group.
Location: England and Wales. Time period: 2011

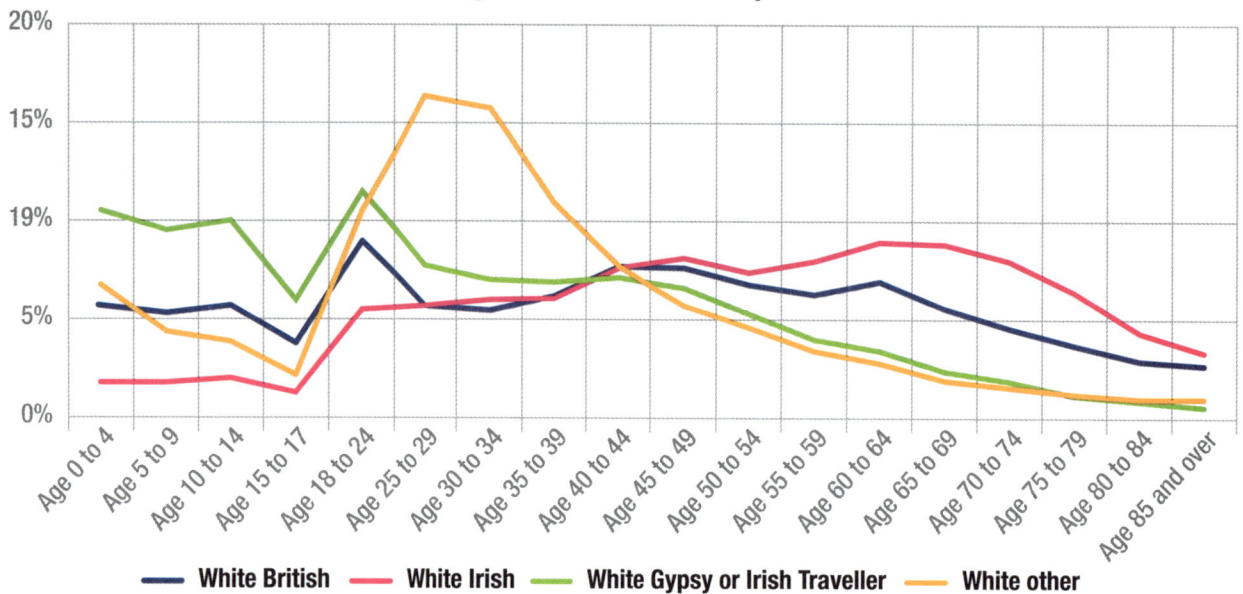

Y-axis: 20%, 15%, 19%, 5%, 0%

X-axis: Age 0 to 4, Age 5 to 9, Age 10 to 14, Age 15 to 17, Age 18 to 24, Age 25 to 29, Age 30 to 34, Age 35 to 39, Age 40 to 44, Age 45 to 49, Age 50 to 54, Age 55 to 59, Age 60 to 64, Age 65 to 69, Age 70 to 74, Age 75 to 79, Age 80 to 84, Age 85 and over

Legend: — White British — White Irish — White Gypsy or Irish Traveller — White other

Source: England and Wales 2011 census / Ethnicity facts and figures GOV.UK

From the graph above, identify the following:

1 Most common age of white other citizens

2 Most common age of white British citizens

3 Least common age of white Irish citizens

4 Least common age of white Gypsy or Irish traveller

Education

Attainment 8 Score

Ethnic group	Score
Asian	50.4
Bangladeshi	50.4
Indian	56.3
Pakistani	45.7
Black	45
Black African	47.5
Black Caribbean	39.6
Chinese	64.2
Mixed	47.3
White	46.1

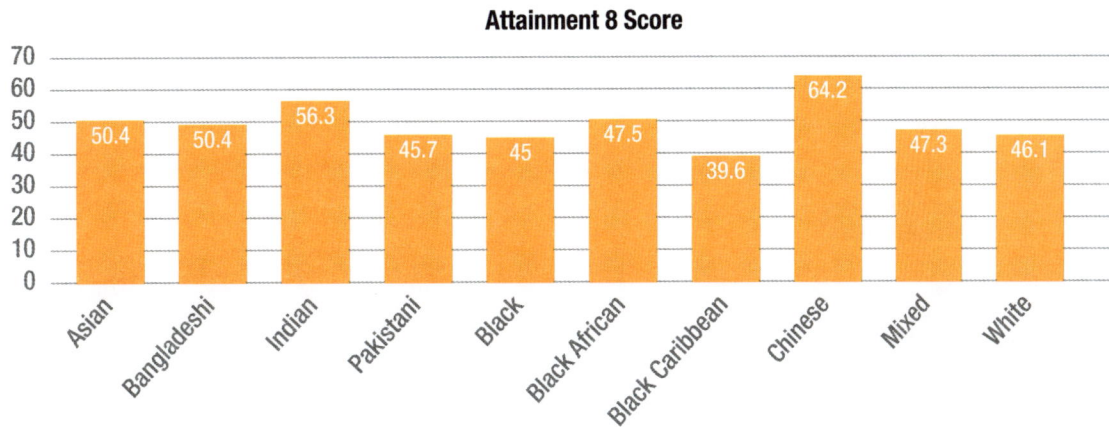

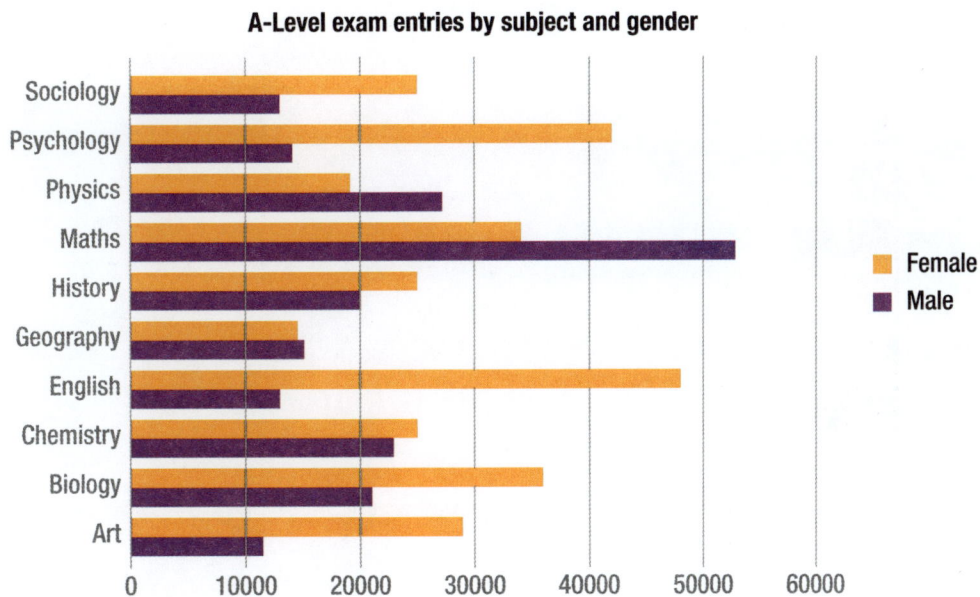

From the bar chart above, identify the following:

1 The ethnic group with the highest attainment 8 score

2 The ethnic group with the lowest attainment 8 score

3 The attainment 8 score of black African students

4 The attainment 8 score of mixed ethnicity students

5 The difference between the attainment 8 scores of Chinese and white students

6 The attainment 8 score of Pakistani students

A-Level exam entries by subject and gender

Subjects (top to bottom): Sociology, Psychology, Physics, Maths, History, Geography, English, Chemistry, Biology, Art

Legend: Female, Male

X-axis: 0, 10000, 20000, 30000, 40000, 50000, 60000

From the bar chart above, identify the following:

1 Most popular male subject

2 Most popular female subject

3 The subject with the least male entries

4 The subject with the least female entries

5 The subject with greatest difference between male and female entrants

NOT LICENSED FOR REPRODUCTION - PLEASE DO NOT COPY THIS BOOKLET **www.tutor2u.net 49**

Crime

**Stop and search rate per 1,000 people, by ethnicity. Location: England and Wales.
Time period: 2017/18**

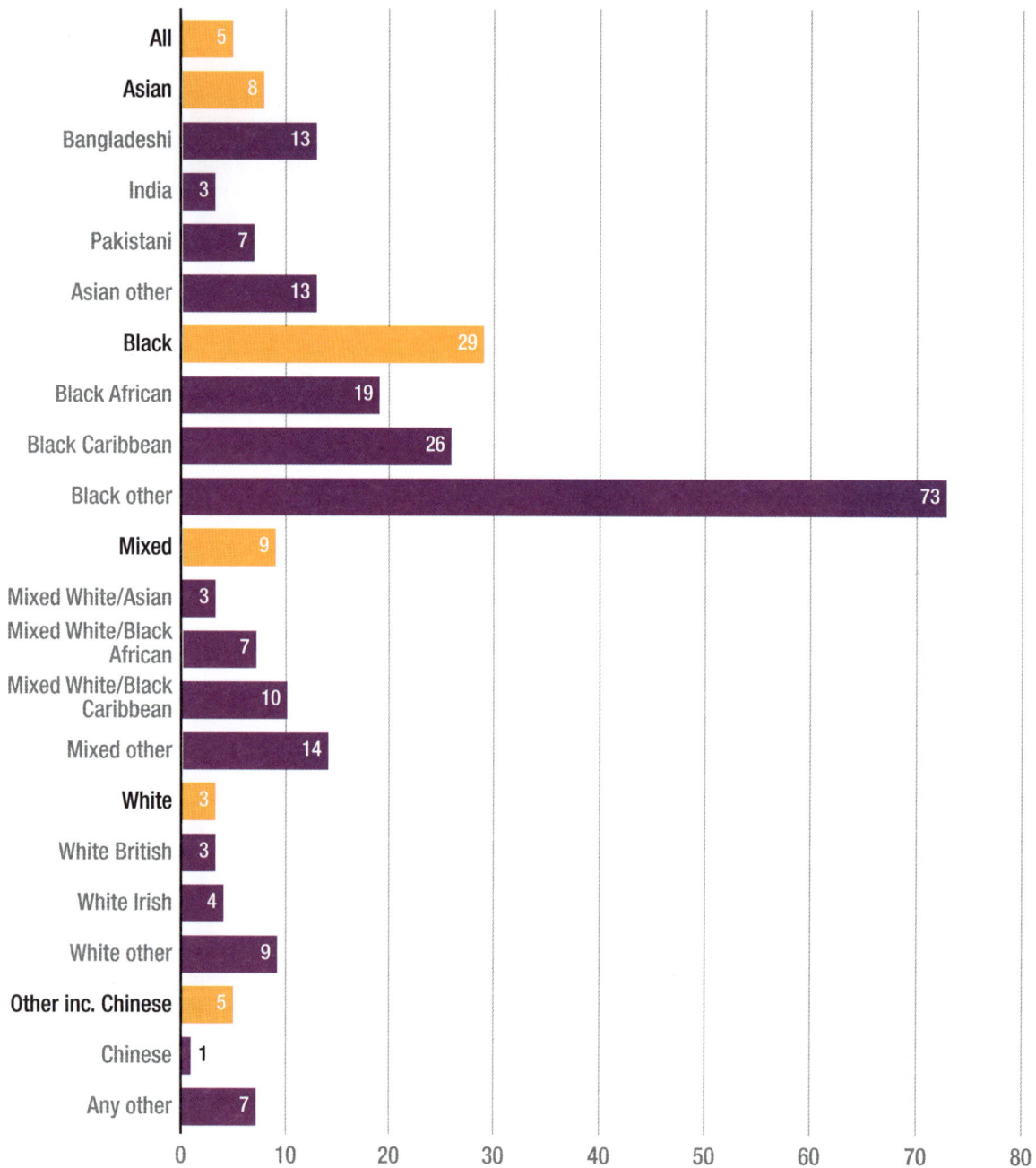

All	5
Asian	8
Bangladeshi	13
India	3
Pakistani	7
Asian other	13
Black	29
Black African	19
Black Caribbean	26
Black other	73
Mixed	9
Mixed White/Asian	3
Mixed White/Black African	7
Mixed White/Black Caribbean	10
Mixed other	14
White	3
White British	3
White Irish	4
White other	9
Other inc. Chinese	5
Chinese	1
Any other	7

Source: Police powers and procedures England and Wales statistics / Ethnicity facts and figures GOV.UK

From the chart, identify:

1 The ethnic group least likely to be stopped and searched

2 The ethnic group most likely to be stopped and searched

3 The rate of white people per 1000 that are stopped and searched

4 The difference between the lowest group to be stopped and searched and the highest.

Stratification

Great British social class survey, % of population in each social class

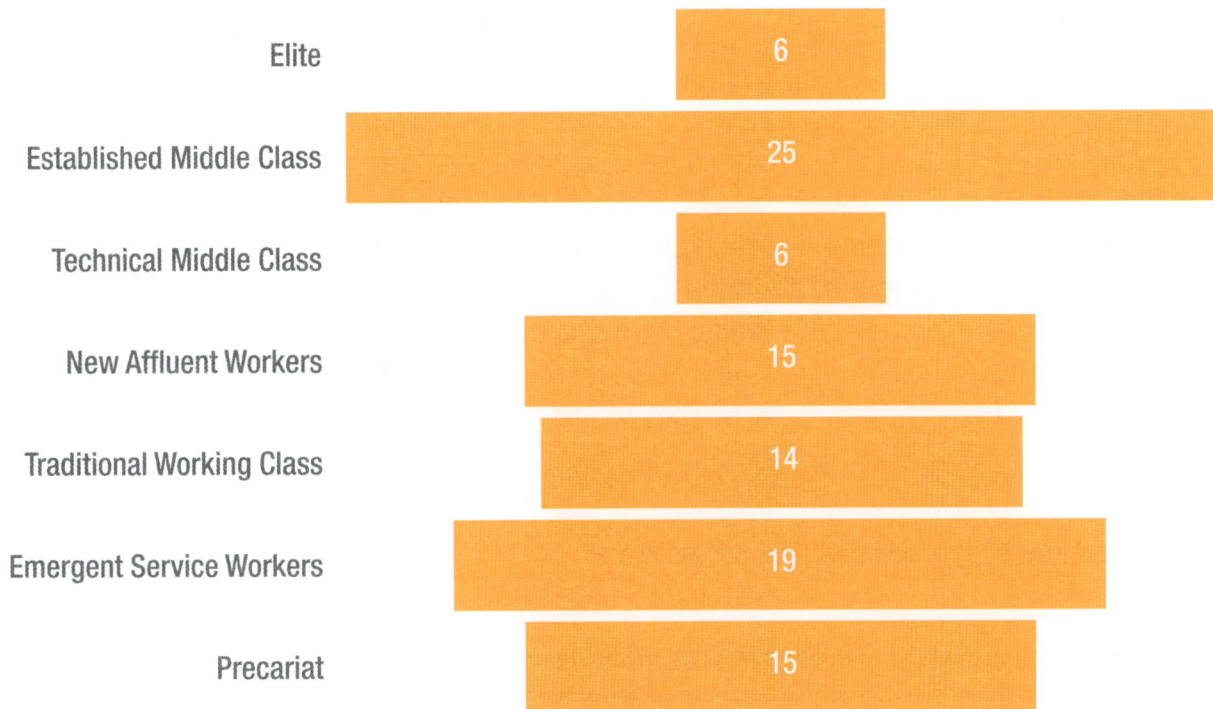

Social Class	%
Elite	6
Established Middle Class	25
Technical Middle Class	6
New Affluent Workers	15
Traditional Working Class	14
Emergent Service Workers	19
Precariat	15

From the chart, identify:

1 The most common social class in Britain

2 The least common social class in Britain

3 The percent of the population who are classed as traditional working class

4 The percent of the population classed as precariat

6 PRACTICAL ISSUES

Sociologists' choice of research method is influenced by practical issues, ethical issues and theoretical issues. Practical issues relate to time, money and access to participants. Sometimes the best method for researching a particular topic, theoretically, has to be rejected because it would cost a great deal of money to conduct, it would be very difficult to carry out, or because it would take a very long time to get results. For instance, researchers considering social change would often consider a longitudinal study, however the funding body supporting the research may be reluctant to fund such a study as they would prefer to see a timely return on their investment.

The main practical issues to consider for GCSE Sociology are:

Time

How long will it take to conduct the research? What deadlines might a sociologist have to meet? What aspects of the research process might take the most time to complete? What type of data will be quickest to analyse? What will be the quickest way to distribute questionnaires or conduct interviews?

Money

Who will fund the research? Which method might be the most cost effective? What will be the costs of hiring equipment? How much training will other researchers require? How many research assistants might be required to collate the data? Will any specialist qualifications be required for the researcher to gain access?

Access

How will the researcher access the participants? What type of sampling method might they have to use to gain a representative sample? How will they access hard-to-reach groups? Will they be able to access certain places, such as schools and care homes, that require DBS checks?

In the table on the following page, consider the practical issues of time, money and access for each of the methods that you have studied throughout this booklet.

Consequences	Issues with time	Issues with money	Issues with access
Questionnaires			
Interviews			
Observations			
Experiments			

7 ETHICAL ISSUES

When sociologists carry out research, they must consider ethics: problems that relate to the morality of the research or research method. This includes whether the research method requires any deception and that participants have given their full informed consent to their contribution. It includes the issue of whether the research could cause any discomfort or harm, or indeed whether it includes any illegal activity. Furthermore, there are issues of participants' anonymity and privacy.

Before a sociologist can conduct their research, they need to submit their research proposal to an ethics committee. This is a board of sociologists that will examine the proposal and suggest any amendments to the research if they believe it to be in breach of the British Sociological Association's ethical guidelines. Researchers should consider:

- How they are going to gain informed consent for their research?
- Will the research cause those being researched any physical or psychological harm?
- How they are going to protect the confidentiality of the research participants?

Some methods of research may breach one or more of these guidelines. It is up to the ethics committee to decide whether these breaches are necessary in order to obtain results.

For GCSE Sociology the key ethical issues are:

Consent

Informed consent refers to the practice of asking a participant permission and providing them with the aims and objectives of the research. Whilst not applicable to all research methods, achieving informed consent from participants is seen as being ethically appropriate.

Often consent can be achieved at the end of the research. In some instances, presumptive consent can be given by an ethics committee if they believe that requesting informed consent from the participants would put the aims of the research at risk.

With some methods, such as interviews and questionnaires, consent is granted by taking part in the questionnaire or interview, and the purpose of the research is clear. With other methods, such as observations, the participants may be unaware they are being observed and therefore have not given their consent. In these cases, consent may be granted after the research, or presumptive consent agreed.

Confidentiality

Confidentiality is the ethical requirement that researchers must keep names and other easily identifiable characteristics out of published research so as not to breach the privacy rights of individuals or groups. This includes the safety and security of data about the participants, which must be kept in accordance with GDPR legislation.

Furthermore, information disclosed during the research must be treated sensitively. Sociologists often research criminal activities and ethically, they must decide if they should report criminal activity to the relevant authorities. This may, however, put their research at risk, and this is a decision that researchers must take seriously. Do they breach their ethical code if it could potentially cause somebody psychological or physical harm?

Harm to Participants

The British Sociological Association set out the duty of researchers to protect their research participants from harm as follows.

'Sociologists have a responsibility to ensure that the physical, social and psychological well-being of research participants is not adversely affected by the research. They should strive to protect the rights of those they study, their interests, sensitivities and privacy, while recognising the difficulty of balancing potentially conflicting interests.'

Source: BSA, 2017

While methods like interviews and questionnaires may seem harmless, researchers must consider the psychological impact of some of the questions they may ask. Questions about family life, domestic violence, being the victim of crime and bullying in education may cause distress to participants, so it is imperative that researchers are able to offer support to those that feel harmed.

Methods such as observations may also cause harm, both to participants and to the researcher themselves, so all precautions must be taken to minimise the risk of harming participants in these circumstances.

In the table on the following page, consider the ethical issues of consent, confidentiality and harm to participants for each of the methods that you have studied throughout this booklet.

Consequences	Consent	Confidentiality	Harm to participants
Questionnaires			
Interviews			
Observations			
Experiments			

KNOWLEDGE CHECK

1   Identify one ethical issue that sociologists might face when investigating anti-school subcultures and explain how you would resolve this in your investigation.   (4 marks)

_____

_____

_____

_____

_____

_____

2   Identify one ethical issue that may arise when conducting unstructured interviews and explain how you would resolve this in your investigation.   (4 marks)

_____

_____

_____

_____

_____

_____

3   Describe one way in which sociologists can ensure that a participant's confidentiality is maintained in research.   (3 marks)

_____

_____

_____

_____

_____

4   Identify and explain one ethical issue with conducting covert observations.   (4 marks)

_____

_____

_____

_____

_____

_____

In this section, we will be examining some of the different types of research methods questions that could appear on the exam. Research methods questions on the GCSE Sociology exam appear in each section of both papers and are placed in the context of the four different topic areas (Families, Education, Crime and Stratification). Methods in context questions require you to apply your knowledge of BOTH research methods and the topic area.

These questions are usually presented with an item or they ask you to identify strengths or limitations of using a research method to investigate an area of family life, education, crime or stratification. On previous papers, these questions have been 1, 2, 3 or 4 marks each and, depending upon the command words in the question, ask you to do different things. Some of the command words used are detailed below:

Multiple Choice

These questions will be presented with the command words **What** or **Which** and will be a simple **identify the right answer** question.

1   Which of the following is an ethical issue? .   (1 mark)

a	Consent	☒
b	Time	☐
c	Access	☐
d	Money	☐

2   What term is used by sociologists to describe the process of people changing their behaviour when they are being observed?   (1 mark)

a	Interviewer bias	☐
b	Hawthorne Effect	☒
c	Longitudinal study	☐
d	Objectivity	☐

Identify and describe (4)

Item A

Willmott and Young developed their ideas about family life, following on from the functionalist ideas of sociologists like Talcott Parsons. From their research (much of it based on social surveys) of families in East London, they developed an idea of the family developing through several stages through history: a march of progress.

They argued that in 1973, families had become symmetrical - that is, that men and women performed similar roles. Rather than the traditional nuclear family described by Parsons where men and women had very separate roles in the family (segregated gender roles) Willmott and Young argued that in modern families men and women both did paid work and both did work around the house, including childcare. They did not find that men and women did the same type of jobs - whether in the workplace or at home - but (compared with earlier periods) family life was becoming more shared and equal. Part of this was also that men and women and children spent more time together in the home rather than separately outside the home (e.g. men going to the pub).

Another important concept for Willmott & Young was stratified diffusion. They argued that changes in norms and values tend to start among the wealthier in society and then others start to behave in the same way (the behaviour is "diffused" from one strata - class - to another).

This led them to a perhaps surprising conclusion that they predicted that the next stage of the family would bet he asymmetric family. They found that richer families spend more time apart and had more segregated roles, with wives not needing to work, and men spending time on the golf course rather than at home. This prediction has clearly not turned out to be accurate, with - if anything - family life becoming more symmetrical since 1973.

> **From Item A, identify and describe the method used by Wilmott and Young including what you know of their perspective on family life.**

This type of question is usually presented with an extract from the research and asks the student to identify the research method that is being used and summarise what they know about the research from the list of required reading.

One mark is awarded for identifying the method – in this case – interviews or questionnaires.

A further three marks are awarded for describing Young and Wilmott's view of family life.

Sample answer:

Wilmott and Young used questionnaires in their research of family life. From a functionalist perspective, Wilmott and Young saw that there was a 'march of progress' towards greater equality in the household, with families becoming more symmetrical as time progressed. They suggest that leisure time, paid employment and household labour was becoming shared and that eventually the working-class family would evolve into an asymmetrical family, copying the family life of the upper and middle classes, due to the principle of stratified diffusion – how culture was passed down from the elites to the workers.

Identify and explain (4)

> **Identify and explain one disadvantage of using official statistics to measure levels of poverty.** (4 marks)

These questions are awarding one mark for identifying a disadvantage and a further three marks for a 'detailed and well-developed explanation of relevant sociological theories, concept and ideas' related to the specific context (poverty).

Sample answer:

One disadvantage of using official statistics to measure poverty is the government's definition of poverty. Townsend in his research disagreed with the official definition of poverty as it did not consider the expenditure that households had, only their income. Instead, he used a measure of relative deprivation that considered people's expenditure, such as food, clothing and bills.

please HELP

From the Item, examine (2)

Item B

James Patrick – Glasgow Gang Observed

Patrick faced many challenges when conducting his research. He had obtained access to the group from a former student but was not always practiced in the ways of the gang. At one point, his role was almost revealed when he paid cash for a suit rather than getting it on store credit. This aroused suspicions amongst the others, who were not used to people having the money to pay for goods upfront.

From Item B, examine one limitation of using covert participant observations to investigate gangs. (2 marks)

In this type of question, you are being awarded one mark for analysing the item and finding a limitation and a further mark for demonstrating knowledge of why this is a limitation of using covert participant observation.

One mark would be awarded for extracting 'maintaining cover' and **one mark** would be awarded for explaining why that was a limitation.

> Sample answer:
>
> *One limitation of using covert participant observation to investigate gangs is always the need to maintain their cover. This is a limitation as, with gangs, the consequences of deceiving gang members could place the researcher at risk of harm.*

Describe, Identify and Explain (4)

Item C

Total divorces UK

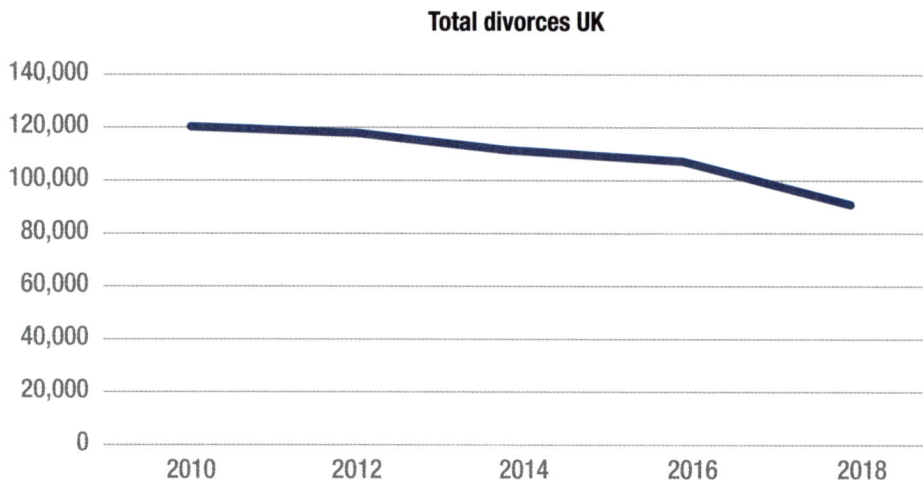

Describe the research method in Item C, **identify** the trend shown by the data, and **explain** one factor that might explain this trend. (4 marks)

This question is split into 3 different command words. 1 mark is being awarded for identifying the research method, a second for identifying the trend and two further marks for explaining one factor that explains the trend.

> Sample answer:
>
> *The research method used in the item is official statistics. The graph shows that there is a downward trend in the number of divorces over the past 8 years. One factor that might explain this trend is the reduction in number of marriages over the past 40 years. With fewer people getting married, there are less married couples to get divorced, hence the decline.*

KEY TERM GLOSSARY

One of the most important skills in studying sociology is being able to use the key terms correctly. Over the following pages some of the key terms that have been mentioned in this booklet are defined.

Key term	Definition
Attitude survey	A social survey that looks to measure the attitudes of people in society through asking questions on social issues. An example of this type of survey is the social attitudes survey conducted on male and female attitudes to housework and the division of labour in the household.
Bias	Bias refers to the inability of a researcher to maintain their objectivity when conducting research. This bias could be based upon preconceived ideas about a social group, or it could be due to a theoretical perspective that the researcher has. For example, both Marxists and feminists would be heavily influenced by the idea that there is conflict in society and clearly choose to side with oppressed groups, such as the working class or females.
Case study	A case study is an in-depth study that can use a variety of different methods, questionnaires, interviews, observations, etc. to study a small sub-section of the population or an individual. This usually takes place over a period of time, and can give a broad range of data about an individual or group.
Closed question	A closed question is one that has a finite number of responses that are usually selected by the researcher and can easily be quantified, and the data extracted and displayed in graphs and charts to show trends.
Confidentiality	Confidentiality is the ethical requirement that researchers must keep names and other easily-identifiable characteristics out of published research so as not to breach the privacy rights of individuals or groups.
Content analysis	Content analysis is a research method that aims to turn qualitative data into quantitative data by categorising the content of articles, films, documents and other secondary sources into easily identifiable themes. The frequency of these themes in secondary sources is then counted and conclusions drawn from the quantitative data.
Covert observation	A covert observation is an observation of participants without their prior consent and without their knowledge that they are being observed. Covert observations can be participant (where the researcher takes part in the group's activities) or non-participant (where they are removed from the group and observe from a distance).
Data	Data refers to the information collected by sociologists when conducting research. This data can be either quantitative (take the form of numbers) or qualitative (in the form of words and images).
Data analysis	Data analysis is the process of understanding the trends and patterns present in data through a systematic examination of the available data.
Data protection	Data protection refers to the legislation that protects the information of individuals and groups that are held by organisations. Legislation such as the Data Protection Act and GDPR dictate ways in which data can be stored and used and breaching these regulations can lead to heavy fines.
Ethical considerations	Ethical considerations refers to the way researchers plan their research to adhere to ethical guidelines about conducting research with human participants. Issues such as deception of participants, protecting participants and the researcher from psychological or physical harm, gaining informed consent, allowing participants the right to withdraw from the research and ensuring privacy and confidentiality are amongst these ethical considerations.
Ethnography	Ethnography is a research methodology that is a systematic examination of a cultural phenomenon whereby the researcher studies the group by viewing society from their point of view. This method is often very high in validity as it enables the researcher to experience what the subjects of their research would experience.
Focus group	A focus group (sometimes referred to as a group interview) is a collection of people from a representative range of the population who are asked questions by a researcher on their beliefs, views and attitudes.
Hypothesis	A hypothesis is an informed prediction that is based upon a limited level of research into a topic area that serves as a starting point for further research.
Informed consent	Informed consent refers to the practice of asking a participant permission and providing them with the aims and objectives of the research. Getting informed consent from participants is seen as being ethically appropriate.

Key term	Definition
Interview	An interview is a conversation between a researcher and a respondent that can be either structured, semi-structed or unstructured. In a structured interview, the researcher will have a specific list of questions to ask (known as an interview schedule) which they will ask the respondent in the same order. An unstructured interview will not have pre-planned questions, just a few headings or aims, allowing for a free-ranging discussion. A semi-structured interview combines elements of both, with an interview schedule that is flexible and allows the researcher to probe further if necessary.
Longitudinal study	A longitudinal study is a research method that involves repeated research of the same group over a long period. This can be achieved through observations, questionnaires or interviews.
Mixed methods research	Mixed methods research refers to the use of a range of different methods to study a topic or issue. Using both quantitative methods and qualitative methods gives a more reliable and valid picture of what a researcher is studying.
Non-participant observation	A non-participant observation is an observation whereby the researcher observes from a distance and does not take part in the activities of the group. This type of observation can be either overt, where the subjects know they are being observed, or covert, where the subjects are unaware that they are being observed.
Observation	An observation is a research method where a researcher observes the behaviour of a group or an individual in order to witness social behaviour. They can be either participant or non-participant. Additionally, each of these types can be overt (where subjects are aware that they are being watched) or covert (where they are unaware).
Open question	An open question is one with an infinite number of responses. Respondents to open questions are usually able to expand on their responses and give more valid and developed responses than in a closed question.
Participan observation	A participant observation is a research method where the researcher is directly involved in the activities of the group and could potentially influence their actions. Whilst this is seen as having greater validity, it could also lead to the research becoming biased in favour of the researcher's hypothesis. Participant observations can either be overt (where the subjects of research are aware that they are being observed) or covert (where the subject are not aware of the intentions of the researcher, nor are they aware they are being observed).
Primary data	Primary data refers to the process of a researcher collecting data first-hand. By using primary data, the researcher can be more certain that the data they are looking for fits the criteria for their research. Examples of primary data could be experiments, questionnaires, interviews and observations.
Qualitative data	Qualitative data is data , usually in the form of text, that describes opinions, views, motivations or meanings of the people that are researched. Qualitative data offers a researcher more insight into the lives of those they study.
Quantitative data	Quantitative data is data that is represented in the form of numerical data. Quantitative data can be drawn from responses to closed questions through coding questions or could be collected through opinion polls measuring intentions or statistics, such as census data.
Questionnaire	A questionnaire is a list of questions that are usually presented in a written format to respondents. They can be open (infinite responses), closed (finite responses) or mixed. Questionnaires can be administered via email, through post, given to respondents to complete in their own time and return, or with a researcher present.
Quota sample	A quota sample is a sampling method whereby the researcher looks to include a certain number of people from a range of categories to make the research as representative as possible. For example, if the researcher is looking for 100 participants and 11% of the population are from non-white ethnic groups, the researcher may look to recruit 11 of their participants from non-white ethnicities to ensure that all groups in society are represented. Therefore, they would wait until they have 11 participants from non-white ethnicities and select 89 people from white ethnic groups.
Random sample	A random sample is one where every person on the sampling frame has an equal chance of being selected for the research. This is seen as representative as names are either simply drawn from a hat or allocated by a random number generator.
Reliability	Reliability is a term used in research methods to explain whether a piece of research can be repeated with different participants and gain a similar result. Quantitative methods tend to be higher in reliability than qualitative ones, as qualitative methods usually measure a person's understanding or insight, which is likely to differ from one person to the next.